THE BOY WHO BIKED THE WORLD

Part Two: Riding the Americas

ALASTAIR HUMPHREYS

ILLUSTRATED BY TOM MORGAN-JONES

Published by Eye Books

Published in 2014
by Eye Books Ltd
29 Barrow Street
Much Wenlock
Shropshire
TF13 6EN

www.eye-books.com

ISBN: 978-1-903070-87-1

Journal typeface based on Grace McCarthy-Steed's handwriting

British Library Cataloguing in Publication Data
A catalogue record for this book is available from the British Library

Printed by CPI Group (UK) Ltd, Croydon CR0 4YY

For Ben and Jack

Contents

Tom's Route Round the World

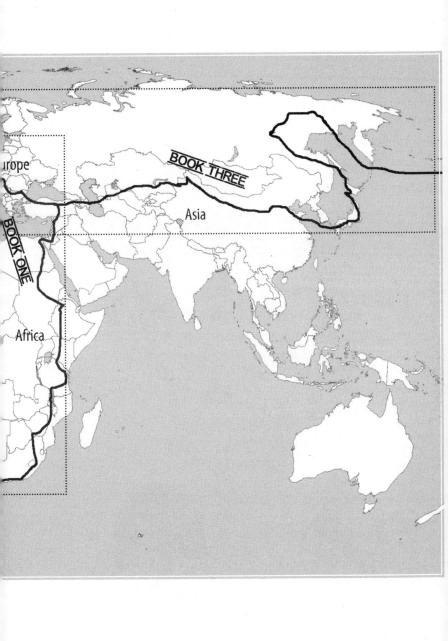

BANANA CRISIS
ON THE HIGH SEAS

Tom was sweating. He was nervous. Really nervous. He jiggled up and down, fidgeting from one foot to the other. If you were looking at Tom, you might have thought that he was desperate for the toilet. But this was even more serious than that! Tom was in a hurry, perhaps the biggest hurry he had ever been in. And nobody seemed to care. It appeared – as he bobbed up and down looking at his watch every single second – that everybody was moving in slow motion.

A man strolled about, looking as though he had not a care in the world. A lady was *standing still* and shaking her shoulders to the beat of the music in her headphones. Standing still! How could anyone have the time to just stand and stare in one place?! Oh dear, oh dear, thought poor Tom. I really am in trouble now. I really am late ...

In front of him was the cause of Tom's problems. A little old lady. To anyone else, she appeared to be a nice, kind, slightly slow old lady. A little bit like your own Grandma, perhaps. Tom was behind her in the queue and she was taking an age to pay for her shopping.

"Come on!" screamed Tom inside his head. "Hurry up! Please!"

He was too polite to actually shout this out loud, though he very much wanted to. He was trying everything he could think of, all his superhero powers of firing laser beams from his eyes or shrinking her to the size of an ant, or making her explode. But nothing he did seemed to work. Because Tom did not have any super powers. He was just a normal boy. The little old lady was in absolutely no hurry. Tom's journey round the world was about to come crashing to a halt. He couldn't decide whether to scream or to cry. So instead he just jiggled a bit more, sweated a bit more, and looked at his watch again and again.

He was going to miss the boat.

"Don't miss the boat, young Tom!" were the last words Captain Horrocks had said. "We can't wait: we leave at high tide."

Captain Horrocks was about to sail across the Atlantic Ocean on his small yacht, *Damsel*. He had kindly invited Tom to join his crew on the adventurous crossing from Africa to South America.

Tom had set off from his home to try to ride his bike all the way round the world. He had already pedalled from England to South Africa. Now he needed to get across the ocean so that he could cycle up the Americas. Tom didn't want to travel by aeroplane – there is no adventure on an aeroplane, only soggy food and annoyingly small TV screens. So Captain Horrocks' invitation to sail to South America was an exciting opportunity. The chance might not come again.

Captain Horrocks and his crew had been hard at work to get the boat ready. Everything needs to be in good condition before you set out to cross an ocean. They repaired everything that was broken, checked the sails, checked them a second time, tested the water-maker that turns seawater into drinking water, and stocked the boat with piles of food. Everything was ready. Everything, that is, until Captain Horrocks remembered that they had forgotten to buy bananas.

"Batter my barnacles!" shouted the captain, who enjoyed a colourful selection of seaworthy swear words. "We can't head out to sea without bananas!"

"Grease my jellyfish!" he continued. His face was red with anger behind his bushy white beard. "Which fool was in charge of shopping?"

"Errr … *you* were in charge of shopping," replied Sailor Sam but quietly, for he was scared of the captain's anger.

This took Captain Horrocks by surprise. It was *his* fault that there were no bananas on board. Suddenly he looked embarrassed rather than cross. The captain waved his arms around a bit more and looked at his crew, hoping to catch someone's eye and think of a reason to shout at them. But all the sailors were looking at the floor, or looking at their fingernails as though fingernails were suddenly very interesting indeed. They knew, through years of sailing the high seas with Captain Horrocks, that they should never catch his eye when he was cross.

As Captain Horrocks couldn't find anybody to shout at instead he said quietly and politely,

"Young Tom, would you be so kind as to run along and buy bananas, please? We need *a lot*."

Tom was delighted! He had been worried about the lack of bananas – they were his favourite adventure food.

"Of course! I *love* bananas."

"Excellent. But make sure you're quick. We set sail in an hour. We won't be able to wait for you if you're late."

And that is how Tom ended up fretting and fidgeting in the checkout queue at the supermarket. He had filled a trolley (one of those really big ones) with nothing but bananas. He piled them as high as he could, a huge teetering, tottering pile of lovely yellow fruit. Tom was standing in the queue waiting to pay whilst the little granny rummaged ever so slowly through her purse looking for her money.

At long, long last the invisible daggers and laser beams that Tom had been firing from his eyes seemed to do the trick. The old lady found the coin she had been searching for, paid for her little basket of shopping and left. Tom emptied his pockets of all the South African money he had, paid in seconds, and sprinted back to the boat. It's hard to sprint when you're carrying hundreds of bananas, but that day Tom managed it.

He arrived just as Sailor Sam was loosening the ropes that tied the boat to the shore.

"I didn't think you were going to make it!" Sam laughed.

Tom was too out of breath to speak. His chest heaved and he was panting like a dog. Passing the bananas onto the boat, he jumped aboard. The boat edged away from the harbour wall, and Tom smiled. They were off! He had made it – in the nick of time – and they were on their way. The adventure had begun!

Tom had never sailed across an ocean before, so he had a lot to learn. But there was plenty of time: about 4000 miles of sea lay ahead of them. So on this first day he got busy with one of the most helpful things you can do on a busy sailing boat: not getting in anybody's way!

People were hauling ropes, heaving armfuls of heavy flapping sails into position and shouting a lot. The bananas were tied in big bunches out of the way at the back of the boat. They were next to Tom's trusty bike and gear. Tom's panniers (the bags that attach to his bicycle) held everything that he would need for his trip around the world. Battered and dusty, they had come a long way since he left England. Tom sat on the edge of the boat – known as the gunwale (rhymes with "tunnel" and has nothing to do with either guns or whales) – dangling his legs over the whooshing blue waves.

Tom looked back at the city they were leaving behind. He could see cars driving along the roads and people sitting in the cafés that lined the seashore. Cape Town was the most beautiful city he had seen so far on his journey round the world. He saw a girl eating an ice cream and waving at the boats. Tom waved back at her.

"I wish I had an ice cream," he thought. It was hot under the big African sun. "I really, really wish I had an ice cream."

What Tom did not know was that the girl was thinking to herself at that very same moment, "I really, really wish I was out there on that sailing boat."

Above the cafés on the shore was a cluster of tall skyscrapers, their windows glinting in the sunshine. And behind the skyscrapers soared the impressive sight of Table Mountain. If you see a picture of Table Mountain, you can easily recognise it, as it has a flat top like a table. Sailors can see Table Mountain almost 100 miles out at sea. It is one of the oldest mountains in the world, more than 600 million years old.

There is an animal that is very common on the mountain called a dassie. It looks a bit like a guinea pig. But its closest relative is actually an elephant!

The waves' spray soaked Tom and he licked the salty taste of the sea from his lips. The yacht was leaning over on its side now, "heeling", as the wind pushed against the sails. But what was this? He became aware of a strange feeling in the pit of his stomach. A sort of squelchy, gurgling-type feeling.

Yes, something very odd was happening down there in his tummy. Something not very nice at all.

"I think," Tom muttered to himself, "I think … I think I am going to be …

BLEEARGGGGHH!"

Without any warning, Tom was sick. He leaned forward and heaved as his lunch – chewed up and disgusting-looking – came spewing out of his mouth and into the sea. Seasickness is caused by the movement of a boat rocking up and down. Some people get the same sick feeling in cars. Tom felt horrible.

Captain Horrocks was steering the boat, heaving the massive steering wheel from side to side to keep the boat straight amongst the bouncing waves.

"Are you OK, young Tom?" he shouted into the wind.

"Ugh …" was all the boy could reply.

"Well, flip my flying fish! You're seasick, aren't you?"

"Ugh …"

"Your face is as green as a Brussels sprout!"

"Ugh …"

Tom could not be certain, but he thought that Captain Horrocks might be trying to hide a smile …

And at that very moment –

BLEEARGGGGHH!

Tom was sick again. He couldn't believe how much disgusting stuff was coming out of his stomach. And there was no hiding it now – the skipper was laughing very loudly indeed!

"Ho! Ho! Ho!" laughed Captain Horrocks who, with his big tummy and bushy white beard, did look a bit like an ocean-going Father Christmas. "It's very mean of me to laugh at you when you're being sick, young Tom. I'm sorry. Boil my bosun, I know how horrible it can feel."

"Ugh …"

"I'm only laughing because I remember the first time I set out to sea. I was sick as a dog and green as a cabbage. But by the morning you'll be fit as a kipper, I promise you."

"Ugh …" replied Tom. And he crawled down below deck to his bunk bed.

But it was true.

As the sun rose the next morning, Tom was relieved to notice that his stomach, like the ocean, was calmer.

"Fry my flippers!" shouted Captain Horrocks, with a twinkle in his eye. "You be looking much happier today!"

Their boat was out of sight of land now. All around was nothing but enormous, empty ocean.

"I feel *much* better, thank you," answered Tom. "Being seasick is terrible. But now I am very, *very* hungry …"

Captain Horrocks laughed.

"We'll have ourselves a feast of a breakfast, my boy," he said. "And then we'll set about turning you into a proper sailor. How does that sound?"

"Fantastic!" cried Tom, with a big smile.

KIT LIST

Here's a list of all the stuff that
I had with me on my adventure through
the Americas:

1 Bike
2 Panniers
3 Tool kit
4 Puncture kit & pump
5 Helmet
6 Tent
7 Sleeping bag & mat
8 camping stove, pan & spoon
9 Food & water
10 One pair spare pants, socks & shirt
11 Waterproof coat
12 Woolly hat & gloves
13 Sunhat
14 Torch
15 Toothbrush
16 First-aid kit
17 Diary & pen
18 Map & compass
19 Camera
20 Passport
21 Teddy

Map of the Americas

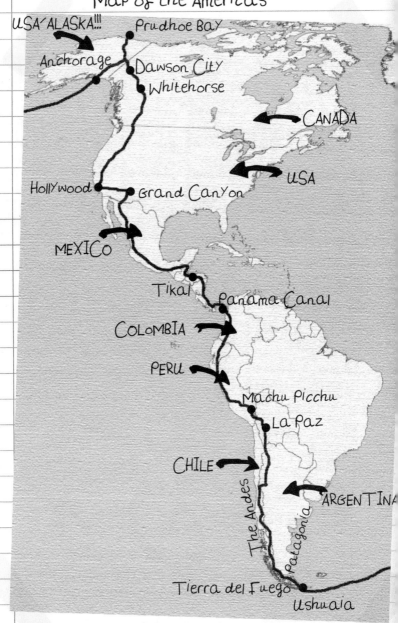

USA' ALASKA!!!

Prudhoe Bay

Anchorage

Dawson City

Whitehorse

CANADA

USA

Hollywood

Grand Canyon

MEXICO

Tikal

Panama Canal

COLOMBIA

PERU

Machu Picchu

La Paz

CHILE

The Andes

Patagonia

ARGENTINA

Tierra del Fuego

Ushuaia

PATAGONIA: LAND OF BIG-FOOTED GIANTS

"**A**laska: 17,848 km." Tom looked up at the signpost and sighed. Alaska was his final destination. And 17,848 kilometres sounded a very long way to cycle. It was a very long way – more than 11,000 miles, more than a third of the way around the globe.

It had been a thrilling moment when, after weeks at sea, Sailor Sam shouted, "Land ahoy!"

Everyone on the boat had turned to look; the first sighting of land is always exciting for sailors. Hills! Trees! Other people! They had made it safely across the Atlantic Ocean. Tom had waved goodbye to the crew and grizzled old Captain Horrocks, then climbed onto his trusty bicycle. It was time to ride! But when you spend weeks at sea, your legs get a bit wobbly. It takes a while before you can walk normally on dry land again. It's even harder to cycle. So Tom weaved and wobbled as he pedalled away from his friends on the boat.

Now, looking up at the signpost, the thrill of being on land was fading. There was just so much land! Tom's plan was to ride from the bottom of South America all the way up to North America and eventually to Alaska, further than he had ever cycled before. His legs felt tired just thinking about it. Surely a normal boy couldn't cycle that far? Tom wasn't a superhero. He wasn't really strong. He was just a boy.

The signpost was on *Tierra del Fuego* in Patagonia – Spanish for "Land of Fire". It got the name because the first European explorer to arrive here saw from his ship the campfires of the Yaghan people who lived here. The explorer's name was Ferdinand Magellan. He believed that the native people who could survive in this wild land at the very bottom of the world must be giants, at least twice as big as normal humans. The name "*Patagonia*" means "Big Foot": this was, Magellan imagined nervously, a land of giants with huge feet.

Patagonia ... The Land of Big-Footed Giants ... The Land of Fire … This was going to be some adventure! Like Magellan, Tom felt nervous himself.

Patagonia is the land right at the bottom of South America. It spans two countries, Argentina and Chile. But the borders between countries were invented long after mountain ranges and mountain tracks appeared. So, for the next few thousand miles of his 17,848 km journey, Tom would be zig-zagging in and out of both Argentina and Chile.

He sat by the sea and ate a banana sandwich, thinking about the distance that lay ahead. Booming waves burst upon the pebble beach. The strong wind tugged at his clothes and messed up his already messy hair. An albatross – the bird known as the king of the oceans because of its three-metre wingspan – circled effortlessly overhead, gliding through the wild wind. Tom gazed out to sea. The cold grey-green water seemed to stretch southwards forever. There were no cities or trees or flowers across that ocean. Across the ocean lay only Antarctica and the South Pole. Tom could see why this tip of South America was described as the End of the World – *El Fin del Mundo*.

He looked up at the albatross. Albatrosses can fly the whole way round the world. The fastest one took just 46 days to do it: much, much less time than it was going to take Tom on his bicycle. Tom called up to the albatross.

"Good morning, Mr Albatross, Mr Albert Ross. Please can I call you Albert?"

He felt a bit silly talking to a bird, but there wasn't another person for miles and miles and miles. So he kept talking.

"Albert," Tom continued, "I'm on a journey round the world, just like you. I'm going to be the boy who biked the world. I need to cycle to Alaska and I'm really nervous. It's so far. I don't think I can do it."

Albert swooped down a little closer.

"I'll be OK, won't I?"

Tom probably imagined it, but he was sure that the great bird winked at him and waggled his wings as if to say, "You'll be fine, young man. Just get started – that is always the hardest part. Begin. Go! Go now, and find yourself a fabulous adventure!"

Tom knew that if he imagined having to ride 11,000 miles then he would probably be too scared to do it. Instead, he had to think only about riding the very first mile. Tom knew that he could ride for one mile. That was easy and definitely not scary. And once he had ridden that mile? Well, then he would ride a second mile, and then a third mile and then a fourth mile. And on and on he would ride, mile by mile, gradually nibbling away at the 11,000-mile journey. If something feels too hard to do, then just take the very first tiny little step. "One mile? That's easy," Tom said to himself. "So don't be too scared to begin. Just go!"

He smiled and climbed onto his bike. He fastened his helmet, then pushed down hard on the pedals. Tom was on his way! The next stage of his adventure had begun! He could not have known it that first morning, but ahead were hot deserts and mountains higher than he had ever seen. He would push his bike through deep rivers and muddy forests. He would even visit a country that enjoyed eating guinea pigs. This was going to be the most difficult, the most exciting part so far of Tom's journey to become the boy who biked the world.

Just for the fun of it, Tom shouted at the top of his voice, "Alaska! Ready or not, here I come!"

But his voice sounded tiny in the emptiness and,

for a moment, he felt lonely out there all by himself. Tom cheered himself up by telling the only joke he knew about Alaska. It wasn't very funny – it was one of his Dad's. But it was better than nothing.

"Where does your Mum come from?"

"Alaska."

"Don't worry, I'll ask her myself …"

By the afternoon Tom was tired because sitting on the sailing boat all the way across the ocean had made him really unfit. He would get fit again in the next few weeks, but right now his legs were aching and his bum was sore, bouncing up and down on this bumpy track! He began looking around for a good place to pitch his tent. After spending weeks at sea where his bed was always wet and every wave battered and bounced him around as he slept, he was looking forward to a dry, still night's sleep.

That first evening, Tom camped by a lake in a soft field filled with yellow and white flowers. From his tent he could see the tops of jagged black mountains dotted with patches of white snow. The only sound, as he drifted off to sleep, was a noisy toad croaking happily in his hole beside the tent.

Patagonia is one of the windiest places on Earth. The wind howls across the ocean, building up speed and power for thousands of miles until it slams into the only bit of land that juts far enough south to get in the wind's way. Wind is a cyclist's biggest enemy. It's worse even than riding up hills. Hills are hard work on a bike. You huff and puff and sweat as you creep up them. But at least you get the fun part of zooming down the other side.

Wind is even worse than the annoying dogs that chased after Tom in many countries, snarling and snapping at his heels. Tom had learned a trick for getting rid of these: he squirted them with water from his drinks bottle and then pedalled away as fast as he could. Headwinds are much, much worse. When the wind blows into your face it slows you down and makes riding really hard work. It pushes you around like a bully, flicking your face, shouting in your ear. A headwind is stupid and dumb – just like a real bully – and is very, very annoying.

One day the wind was so strong that Tom could not even cycle; he had to walk down the road pushing his bike. That was a terrible day. Later the wind became so fierce that it took all his strength not be blown backwards. He had to shelter in a ditch until the wind dropped and he could continue creeping forwards. By late afternoon Tom could still see the place he had set off from that morning. Have you ever travelled that slowly?

Alaska felt a very long way away.

But that evening, as he pitched his tent on a hill looking down over the sea, Tom could still enjoy the feeling of being out in the wild, far from the nearest town or person. Dolphins leaped out at sea and a rainbow hung in the sky. The best part was that Tom got to meet a penguin. He had never seen one in the wild before. After cooking his tea, Tom walked down to the beach to visit a colony of King Penguins.

King Penguins are the second biggest penguins, behind Emperor Penguins. They grow up to a metre tall and have beautiful yellow markings around their faces and throats. The birds waddled up close, curious to take a look at this funny-looking boy creature. They themselves looked funny to Tom as they tottered along the beach, because penguins are not very good at walking. But in the water, they look amazing. King Penguins dive to catch fish, and have even dived as deep as 300 metres. This is three times deeper than any human has dived while holding their breath.

On the previous leg of his journey, when Tom had ridden through Africa, every day had been boiling hot. It was horrible. Sometimes his head got so hot that he thought it was going to burst. Tom dreamed of dropping ice cubes down his pants or swimming in icy seas. He promised himself he would never moan again about cold weather.

Or so he thought …

Because the next morning, here in Patagonia, he woke to an unfamiliar feeling. It was dark in the tent, much darker than it should have been at this time of the morning. During the night it had snowed and Tom's tent was now completely covered, making it dark inside. As he crawled out of his warm sleeping bag, he began to grumble. By the time he had put on his cold shoes and packed away his snow-covered tent, his teeth were chattering.

"I'm f-f-f-f-freeezing!" he shouted, even though nobody could hear him. Except the penguins. They didn't look cold at all. In fact, the penguins looked quite warm and happy in the snow. He thought maybe he should p-p-p-pick up a penguin and use it like a hot water bottle.

"This is t-t-t-terrible!" Tom moaned.

At that moment, he made a new promise. Being cold was so bad that he wished only to be hot. He would never complain again about being too hot. Never ever again!

Tom set up his tiny stove to cook some porridge and ate breakfast straight from the pan. He did the washing up by licking the pan and the spoon until they were clean. He thought back to his life before this adventure began. It felt so long ago now. He used to eat cornflakes for breakfast, or choose from about five other different cereal packets. Or sometimes he would choose toast. He used to really annoy his Dad by taking so long to decide whether to have jam or Marmite on his toast. It had seemed so important back then. These days Tom ate the same thing for breakfast every day – gloopy porridge. It had no real flavour but it was cheap, hot and full of energy. These were the most important things for a meal to be these days. He stirred the porridge and sighed as the gloopy bubbles rose to the surface, then shovelled his breakfast into his mouth very quickly.

Tom zipped his coat up tight, pulled on gloves, and set off as fast as he could to get warm again.

"Goodbye!" he shouted to the penguins, but they didn't reply. Perhaps they didn't understand English.

ADVENTURES IN THE ANDES

O ccasionally Tom passed a lone farmhouse, miles from any other building. It must be peaceful to live out here, he thought. But it might get a bit boring or lonely too. Whenever a farmer spotted Tom he would invite him inside for a bowl of soup and a drink of *mate*. *Mate* ("mar-tay") is the South American version of a cup of tea. *Mate*, though, is always drunk through a silver straw from a ball-shaped cup. Everyone shares the same cup and the same straw, passing them on to the next person. *Mate* is a drink to share and an excuse to have a long chat with your friends. In every country around the world, the people Tom met were kind, curious, generous and welcoming. Patagonia was no exception.

This was one of the most beautiful regions he had ever cycled through. It was wild and free and unfamiliar – the very things that, for Tom, made for the most thrilling adventures. Sometimes the road ran through valleys, sometimes it climbed high in the mountains clinging to the edge of cliffs. The roads didn't have safety barriers, so if Tom fell off his bike he would also fall off a massive cliff! It was scary riding, but exciting.

Turquoise rivers rushed through green forests. Trout leaped to catch flies. Each night Tom jumped into a river to wash. The rivers flowed down from the mountains, thundering over waterfalls, carrying melted snow. They were freezing. In some parts of the world Tom didn't get to wash for weeks on end, and so he was often quite smelly! A chance to get clean in a mountain stream was too good to miss, even if the cold water did make him scream a bit. Jump in the river, it'll make you shiver!

Green fields carpeted with daisies and dandelions reminded Tom of England. Then a rhea ran across the road, reminding him that he was actually very far from home. The rhea is a huge bird, like an ostrich. It stopped and looked in surprise. It had never seen a boy on a bicycle before! Mind you, Tom had never seen a rhea before. It was taller than Tom himself. Rheas cannot fly but they run really quickly, up to 40 miles an hour! Another evening, as he watched the sun set, a little armadillo trotted hastily past Tom's tent. Armadillos sleep for 16 hours a day, so it was a treat to see one actually out and about, looking for food.

Mountains towered above, jagged like sharp teeth, with mighty glaciers running down from the peaks. Glaciers are formed over hundreds of years as snow is compressed and turns into ice. Glaciers are like enormous rivers of ice, but rivers that move so slowly that you can't see them move.

Three-quarters of all the fresh water in the world is frozen into glaciers. Tom looked up at the end of a glacier – a gigantic wall of ice in a bright blue lake. Every so often a chunk would fall into the water 60 metres below. Gigantic blocks of ice – as big as cars – crashed down into the lake with a sound like an exploding bomb. As they hit the lake they made massive splashes, causing huge waves. It was great fun! Tom settled down with a couple of banana sandwiches to watch the show.

The road now was nothing more than a stony track, and Tom's bags rattled as he bounced along. There were no bridges so sometimes he had to cross rivers. Tom would take off his shoes and socks and roll up his trousers above his knees. Then he would push the heavy bike through the freezing water, taking care not to lose his footing. If he fell over he would not only get very cold and wet and cross, he might also be swept away by the strong current.

After a few more days, the track fizzled out completely. Tom felt alone, but not lonely. He felt excited. He had been riding round the world for a long time now. He was fit and strong. He knew how to repair his bike if it broke down. He knew how to read a map, and how to survive in the wild. This was a wilderness challenge, and Tom was up for it!

For a whole day Tom pushed his bike up a small, steep, muddy footpath. Hour after hour, mile after mile. The forest around him was dark. Sometimes he had to carry his bike and bags, and tripped over rocks and roots. It was exhausting. When he eventually reached the top of the track he saw a tall metal post. It was old and rusty. Nobody had been here for a long time.

On one side of the post was written the word "Argentina". On the other side of the post was written the word "Chile". This was the border crossing between two countries! Tom had crossed 30 international borders on his journey around the world, but this was the first time that the border had ever been on a muddy footpath on top of a hill. There were no barriers or police checkpoints. He was wet, cold and tired, but Tom still had the energy to smile and punch the air.

"Yes!" he shouted to himself. "That's one more country done."

He freewheeled slowly down the track, away from Argentina and into Chile, down towards a lake dotted with small icebergs. He could not go very fast for two reasons. The first was that the track was too rocky to go quickly without shaking his bike to pieces. The second reason was that Tom was now sharing the track with an enormous bull! He didn't know where the bull had come from, and he didn't know where it was going. But he did know that the bull was huge and ferocious-looking. Every so often the bull turned around, looked at Tom, and snorted loudly. He didn't want to shout "hurry up" or try to overtake him on the narrow track. So Tom had to settle for trundling along behind the bull until they reached the lake.

The next morning Tom had a lie-in. He had to wait to catch a boat across the lake to the other side, as it was the only way he could continue heading north. He could lie lazily in his sleeping bag for as long as he wanted. The trouble was that Tom didn't know how long he might have to wait. In fact, *nobody* seemed to know! The boat arrived "about every two weeks", but nobody he asked knew anything more than that. It was a relaxed way of life down in Patagonia. The boat did not come that day, so Tom had a lie-in the next morning too. And the morning after that. He threw stones at icebergs, went and said hello to the bull, and washed his clothes in the freezing lake. He was getting bored sitting beside the lake, waiting.

So Tom was happy on the morning of Day Four when he awoke to the chug-chug sound of a boat. Leaping out of his sleeping bag, he ran to the water's edge, waving and shouting. The captain of the yellow-and-blue boat changed direction in order to come and pick him up. Tom hurried to pack his gear and wheel it down to the lake. Everything he owned, including his house, could pack away into just a few bags, ready to move on to the next adventure. It's surprising how few things you really need in life. The fewer things Tom had, the happier he was.

"¡Hola!" he called to the captain. "¿Cómo está usted, señor? How are you, sir?"

Tom hadn't seen another person for days and was happy to have a chat. He was also looking forward to reaching the town across the lake because he had been rationing his food and was now really hungry.

"¡*Vamos!* Let's go!" cried Tom, heaving his bike on board. "*Tengo hambre.* I'm hungry."

Tom pedalled further north. The huge peaks of the Andes mountains – the biggest in the Americas – rose up ahead of him. They were formed millions of years ago. The plates of the Earth's surface push against each other all the time, extremely slowly but with massive force. Hold your hands out flat in front of you. Touch your fingertips together. Now push them harder and harder together. Eventually they will slide one over the other, buckle downwards, or buckle upwards like a mountain range. This is how mountains "grow". The Andes seemed to buckle halfway to the sky. Tom had never seen mountains as big as these.

He gulped. His legs felt wobbly and weak. The road climbed ever more steeply upwards, past acacia trees and prickly pear cacti before disappearing into the clouds. The mountain pass above him was 5000 metres high. And Tom had to ride over it on his bike!

The road zig-zagged up the twisting bends. Sweat dripped into Tom's eyes. He was panting. It would take about two days to ride up this pass. He didn't think he could do it. His legs were wobbling like a jelly, and he was even hungrier than usual. So, as he always did when things seemed impossible, Tom climbed off his bike and sat down to make a banana sandwich.

In a few bites, the sandwich was gone. Then Tom lay down and folded his hands behind his head. It was time for an after-lunch nap. High in the sky, a condor hovered on the warm thermal air that rose from the valley. Condors – giant vultures – are enormous, almost as big as Tom's friend Albert the albatross. Tom let rip an enormous, noisy burp into the quiet mountain air. When you are alone and cycling round the world you can get away with doing very loud burps.

Back on his bike, as the road climbed, the temperature fell. Even though cycling was hot work, Tom needed to pull on an extra jumper. He was wearing thick gloves, a warm hat under his helmet and both his pairs of socks. Up, down, up, down went Tom's legs. Up, up, up crept his bike. On and on and on he pedalled. Down, down, down crept the distance to the top.

A fox, in its white fur coat, flopped through the snow next to the road. The snow was too deep for it to walk through, so the fox was jumping forward then sinking, jumping forward then sinking. It looked even more tiring than cycling up the big mountain.

Tom remembered the lesson this adventure had taught him: when you think you cannot do something big and difficult, do something tiny and easy instead. Take one little step. Push the pedals round once. You can do that. Push the pedals one more time. Then once more. You can always do one more.

Ever so slowly, Tom realised that the road was beginning to flatten out. He was almost at the top. His head was hurting and his legs were wobbling, but he had made it to the top. Tom had ridden all the way up a 5000-metre mountain pass! There would be more mountain passes to come, but doing the first one is always the most difficult.

He stopped at the top to take a photograph of himself and his bike. Then he quickly put on every piece of spare clothing he had. It's always cold high up in the mountains. Camping last night, Tom had had to light a campfire to help keep himself warm. At the top of the pass it was -20°C, the coldest temperature Tom had ever experienced. He even put his spare pair of pants on top of his hat to help keep his head warm. He looked very, very silly with a pair of pants on his head! But it was too cold to care, and nobody was around to laugh anyway. The boy climbed back onto his bike to enjoy his reward for cycling up the mountain.

His reward was the fun of zooming down the other side!

"Woohoo!" Tom howled, free-wheeling faster and faster. Everything passed in a high-speed blur. He freewheeled downhill for 50 miles! It would take about an hour to go that far in a car, or days if you were walking. Think of a town that is 50 miles away from where you live. And now imagine being able to get there on your bike without even having to pedal! Tom's face was fixed into a grin. Riding downhill was the best bit of cycling round the world!

Would you like to be strong enough to cycle over the immense Andes for month after month? It's easier than it sounds. There is no shortcut or magic potion to getting fit without putting in hours of hard work. But if you ride your bike a lot, or run or swim or play sport regularly, then you will become fit and strong. Tom knew that all children need to do at least one hour of exercise a day (something that gets you tired, hot and out of breath), but he was doing a lot more than that.

HOW TO LIGHT A CAMPFIRE

You need 3 things to light a fire:

- Fuel
- oxygen (air)
- Heat

1. Make sure your fuel is really dry – the best fuel is dead fallen sticks that have got stuck in tree branches.

2. Make a small pile of tiny pieces of fuel called tinder – dry grass or paper is good for this.

3. On top build a pyramid of slightly bigger sticks (thinner than a pencil) called kindling.

4. Remember that a fire needs oxygen so make sure to leave lots of gaps so that air can get in. Light the tinder with a match which will set fire to the kindling.

5 | Once the kindling is burning slowly add thicker bits of wood (or dried llama dung if you have any ...) which will burn for a longer time. If the fire is struggling get down low and blow onto the bottom of the fire as though you were blowing through a straw. <u>Be careful</u> doing this!!

<u>Fires can be dangerous.</u> Here's how to make them safer:

- Clear the ground of leaves and twigs.
- Build a circle of large stones round the fire.
- Make sure you have enough water to put the fire out.
- Hold the match far enough down so you don't burn your fingers.
- Don't run or play near the fire.
- Never leave a fire untended.
- Leave no trace: once the fire is completely out cover the fire pit with debris.

<u>NEVER</u> light a fire without permission!

BOLIVIA: A HIGH, COLD WORLD OF WONDERS

Mile by mile, mountain by mountain, Tom moved northwards through the Andes and into Bolivia. Llamas and alpacas grazed on the thin, yellow grass. He was still high above sea level, but the land became flat again. He had reached an area known as the *altiplano* (from the Spanish words "*alto*" – high – and "*plano*" – flat). Farmers had ploughed tiny fields in the dry earth, each field only about as big as Tom's classroom back at school. The farmers did not have tractors or machines so the work was hard. The men dug the earth while their wives and children weeded the ground, harvested vegetables and gathered firewood for cooking.

Beyond the fields, women with babies strapped to their backs spun wool on spindles as they looked after flocks of alpacas. They were turning the alpacas' wool into wool they could use to knit clothes. The women wore bright ponchos – like thick woollen blankets – striped with colourful patterns.

On their heads they wore small bowler hats, which looked quite funny to Tom.

Tom cycled through villages looking for a shop where he could buy some food. But there were no shops. Life is tough in those cold, poor villages. People make, grow or raise everything they eat. In the end, Tom decided to ask a farmer if he could buy some food. He stopped and lay down his heavy bike. The family in the field stood up, stretched their backs, and stared.

Tom was used to being stared at. He looked different to the people in South America. The best way to stop people staring was to begin chatting. People then realised that he was just a normal boy and not some weirdo from another planet. Tom walked towards the family. He smiled and called out, "*¡Hola!*"

They smiled back. The girl, who was about the same age as Tom, said, "*Hola. ¿Cómo te llamas?* Hello. What's your name?"

"*Me llamo Tom*. I'm called Tom."

"*Me llamo Cava*. And this is my brother Apo, and my Mum and Dad – *Mamá y Papá. ¡Bienvenidos!* Welcome!"

Tom had been learning Spanish. It's the language spoken in most countries on the South American continent. He practised whenever he could, and was getting quite good by now, even if he sometimes had to ask people to speak more slowly.

Cava continued to ask Tom questions. Where are you from? What are you doing here? Why do you have a bicycle?

The boy smiled because he had been asked these same questions so often along his journey. Tom explained that he was cycling round the world by bicycle – "*Estoy dando la vuelta al mundo en bicicleta*". He was English – "*Soy Inglés*". He slept in his tent, ate cheap food, and loved the life of adventure – *aventura*.

"*Tengo hambre y sed,*" Tom said. "I am hungry and thirsty".

He asked their Dad whether he could please buy some food – *comida* – and have some water – *agua*.

"Dear Tom," laughed the Dad. "I don't even have enough food to feed my family. My wife and I never eat lunch so that our children may have food to eat. But you are our friend. So of course we will share ours with you."

"*Amigo*, my friend," Apo smiled. "Why don't you stay in our house tonight? You must be tired after cycling all the way from England. Just help us clear this field and we will be finished for the day. We will have a feast. We will have fun!"

Tom smiled, said thank you, then bent down to help weed the field. They all chattered away and the afternoon passed quickly. After helping to milk their llama, Tom spent the night in the family's small home. They ate and laughed and shared stories about their different lives.

Cava's family was poor and their house was very small. In fact, there was only one room. They cooked on a small fire made from twigs and dry llama dung. The walls were black from smoke. There were two wooden chairs in the room, but no beds. When it was time to sleep, the whole family and

Tom lay on the floor and wrapped themselves in blankets to keep warm.

The night outside was cold and still, and the moon was bright.

The next morning Tom filled his water bottles from the tiny stream behind the house and packed his things ready to continue riding. The family were wrapped in their ponchos to keep off the cold. Their breath steamed and ballooned in the freezing dawn air as they waved, calling out,

"*Adiós*, Tom! Goodbye! *¡Buen viaje!* Have a great trip!"

"*¡Gracias, amigos! ¡Adiós!*" waved Tom.

The family returned to the field to work another hard day. They chatted about Tom. They found it funny that Tom's family didn't own a llama, and they couldn't believe that in his country people bought their food in shops rather than growing it themselves. That day Tom cycled fast, smiling all the way. He was grateful for how kind Cava's family had been. Cava and Apo also felt happy. It had been nice to be able to help somebody else.

Tom was on one of the bumpiest, most annoying roads ever. His bike rattled, everything in his bags rattled, even his poor head rattled. You can get an idea of how bumpy this road was. Try this:

Open your mouth and say "aah", like when you go to the doctor. Now shake your head as fast as you can from side to side. Your voice goes funny, everything looks blurry, your head starts to hurt and you start to worry it might even fall off! That's what Tom's ride felt like every day in Bolivia.

He was in a wild and empty area now. No plants grew. The ground was flat grey gravel. An icy wind whistled across the land. The track was in really bad condition. For days he had to walk, pushing his bike. The wind blasted his face and his hands and feet were numb with cold. When he set his tent up at night, he had to pile rocks around to stop it from blowing away. In the morning all Tom's water bottles had frozen solid. He had to keep them inside his sleeping bag to stop them from freezing.

Bolivia was a hard place to ride through.

The land on the *altiplano* is very dry. So Tom was surprised one day when he saw a small lake in the distance. He was even more surprised when he got close: the lake was green, as green as emeralds!

Rising into the sky behind the lake was a volcano, its summit covered with snow. It was a calm day and the volcano reflected onto the green waters of *Laguna Verde* below. Then Tom spotted steam rising into the air. Curious, he went to see what it was. He found a geyser. The heat beneath the surface of the Earth – the same heat that leads to volcanoes – heats up underground water. As the temperature and the pressure rise, boiling water spurts up. Here, clouds of steam rose high into the cold air. Pools of hot water bubbled like jacuzzis. It was a weird but beautiful place, like being on another planet.

After the green lake, Tom found one that was even stranger: a red lake! The red colour came from tiny red algae in the water. Thousands of pink flamingoes stood on one leg in the shallow red water. Flamingoes were one of Tom's favourite birds. They have really long legs and a long neck shaped like a letter "S". Their pink colour comes from eating algae in a lake.

Among this high, cold world of wonders, the highlight was the *Salar de Uyuni*, the largest salt flat in the world. Millions of years ago it was part of an inland sea. But gradually the water dried up until all that was left was the salt. For 200 miles in every direction there is nothing but dazzling white salt. There are no roads or villages, no trees or animals, not even any insects. Tom pedalled carefully out onto the salt. It felt odd to ride on, crunchy. But the salt was flat and hard and Tom found he could cycle quickly across it. It was much smoother to ride than the bumpy mountain roads he had been on recently.

It would take three days to ride across the *salar*, so Tom carried plenty of food and water because there were no shops or taps or even streams out there. He rode all day, then stopped at sunset to camp. After pitching his tent, Tom went for a walk. He walked for a few minutes away from his tent. He spread out his arms and whirled slowly round and round. In every direction, for as far as he could see, was nothing but flat white salt and an enormous blue sky. It felt as empty and remote as the Atlantic Ocean.

But the ocean is usually noisy and is constantly moving.

The salt plain was so still and quiet that Tom could hear himself blink. Try that yourself now. Be as still and quiet as you can. What can you hear? The wind? A car on the road? The quiet hum of lightbulbs? Tom could hear nothing at all. It was a magical feeling. He turned to look at his little tent. It seemed so tiny, over there in the middle of the salt plain. He felt very tiny himself, and very alone. Darkness was falling, so Tom ran back to his tent. He felt cosier and more comfortable once he wriggled into his sleeping bag. It might look like a strange house to most people, but for a boy biking the world, this tent and this sleeping bag were all he needed to feel at home. Above the tent, a shooting star raced across the dark night sky.

Because everything looked identical out on the salt flat, it was easy to get lost. Tom tried an experiment. He closed his eyes and cycled without watching. You can't normally cycle like this without crashing into something. But here, there was nothing to bang into. So Tom pedalled for 30 minutes without watching where he was going – can you imagine trying that at home?! When he eventually looked up, Tom had veered off course and was riding in totally the wrong direction!

"Woohoo!" he cheered, straightening his course using his compass. The excitement of trying new things and going to new places never goes away. Tom smiled happily as he rode on towards La Paz.

THE WITCHES OF LA PAZ

L a Paz is one of the highest cities in the world. It lies in a massive bowl-shaped dip in the earth, surrounded by mountains. As with many cities in poor countries, a huge shanty town has sprouted up on the outskirts. Almost one million people live here, in homes ranging from small cement blocks to shelters with roofs made of plastic sheets. He thought of his own home in England and felt thankful that he did not have to live in a homemade shelter on the edge of a busy road.

Away from the main roads, the streets in the centre of La Paz were steep and cobbled. Market stalls were squeezed into the narrow streets, adding to the chaos and the noise. Small children had the responsibility of trying to sell the few spare vegetables that their parents had brought to the city from their farms. They needed money to buy the things they could not grow themselves. They crouched on the pavement next to their sacks of carrots, chilies and other vegetables. Some smiled at Tom as he passed; others were too busy trying to make a sale that they didn't have time to chat.

The best place to chat to local people is in a café. Whenever Tom was in a town he always ate in cafés. Banana sandwiches are the food for heroes, but whenever possible, he tried to eat a variety of foods, as he knew that to be really fit and strong it was important to eat a good mixture of fresh foods. Tom usually enjoyed trying new foods in different countries, but still shuddered whenever he remembered the blood and milk mixture or the fly burgers in Africa.

The cafés he ate in throughout South America were simple places, with just a few small tables and plastic chairs. There was always a radio playing loud music, and there was never a menu to choose from. You just ate whatever food had been cooked that day. Often this was a big bowl of chicken soup. When he dug down to the bottom of the bowl with his spoon Tom would find the day's surprise ingredient – perhaps a few pieces of potato, perhaps some chunks of carrot. But one part of the chicken soup was never a surprise: there was always a chicken's foot floating on top! Local people thought this was the best bit (*"una pata de pollo"* in case you ever want to order one yourself ...). They slurped and said "mmmm" as they happily sucked on the scaly foot. Tom was not so keen. But an easy way to make friends in those cafés was to give your chicken's foot to another customer to enjoy.

One of the spookiest places in La Paz was an old witches' market. Many people in Bolivia still believe in ancient medicines, spells and superstitions to bring them luck or to help them recover from illness. The market was a fascinating but quite creepy place. Tom pushed his bike amongst the stalls, squeezing through the noisy crowds as stall owners shouted out the health benefits of whatever they were trying to sell. There were candles and incense to use at funerals. There were sacks filled with dry herbs, piles of leaves and berries, and a dusty pile of old, dead armadillos. These were the ingredients for magic spells. There were also large heaps of dead baby llamas. These had been dried in the hot sunshine until they were shrivelled and flat. Some people believe that if you are building a new house you should bury a dead llama in the foundations to bring good luck to the new home.

Tom shivered. When he put up his tent each night, he definitely didn't want a dead llama nearby, even if it was supposed to bring him luck. It was time to ride. He bought a big bunch of bananas, and pedalled out of La Paz.

THE MARVELS AND MYSTERIES OF PERU

On the border between Bolivia and Peru is Lake Titicaca, one of the highest lakes in the world. Shortly after he arrived, Tom met a man called Sergio on the shore of the lake. Sergio was short and skinny with a sun-weathered, wrinkly face like a raisin. His white teeth shone when he smiled.

Sergio was a boat builder from the Uros people. He built boats for the fishermen who worked on the large lake. Hardly any trees grow in this part of the world because they are too high up, the soil is poor quality, and it gets very cold. So the boat builders of old had to find an alternative to making their boats out of wood. Instead of wood, they used reeds.

Reeds are tall, thick grasses that grow at the shallow edges of lakes and rivers. Sergio had a sharp, curved knife that he used to chop big armfuls of them. Then he wove and tied bundles of the reeds together and shaped them into boats. On Lake Titicaca, not only do people build boats out of reeds, they also build their villages out of reeds, and these float out in the middle of the lake! Sergio invited Tom to visit his island village, and they paddled out to see it on a little reed boat.

To build a floating village, you have to lay down a massive base mattress of reeds. It needs to be thick enough to float, even with homes and people on top. All the homes on the floating base are made from reeds, too. It was a beautiful sight – the lake blue and cold beneath the bright mountain sky; the ladies of the village working in big colourful skirts – green, red, blue – with bowler hats shielding their faces from the sun.

After Tom visited Lake Titicaca, the mountains began again. Up he went, down he went on his bike, day after day after day. Up, down, up, down. *Arriba, Abajo, Arriba, Abajo …* The road was leading Tom towards one of the most famous and beautiful ancient places in the world.

Machu Picchu was built as a royal estate by the Incas 600 years ago. It sits high on a steep, narrow mountain ridge. After the site fell into ruin, it lay forgotten for hundreds of years. By the time the explorer Hiram Bingham discovered the ruins in 1911, it was completely covered in jungle. Tom was excited to climb up to see Machu Picchu for himself, but he was also a bit jealous of Hiram Bingham. Can you imagine how exciting it would be to find a forgotten city hidden in the jungle?

"Wow!" Tom thought, imagining himself hacking through jungle to discover an ancient city.

The buildings at Machu Picchu are made from enormous chunks of stone that fit together perfectly, even though the builders didn't have proper stone-cutting tools. They had to carry the heavy stones all the way up the mountain, without even a wheel to help. As the wheel hadn't been invented yet in South America, they used levers and ropes made from grass. What hard work that would have been! Tom got tired just cycling up to the ancient site. And he had two wheels to help him and no boulders to carry.

As Tom rode on through Peru, he reached one of the most puzzling sites in the world. Nazca is a dry desert area. About 1500 years ago, the Inca people who lived here made a series of lines, shapes and pictures of animals in the desert. They did it by removing the red pebbles that are the surface of the desert and digging a shallow trench. Underneath is earth that is paler in colour, and so it shows up as a line. Because it almost never rains here, the lines have not been washed away over time.

The shapes are huge. There are pictures of a hummingbird, a spider and a monkey, each at least as big as a football pitch. What is most peculiar about these patterns in the desert is that you can only see them from the air. It is a real mystery why the Inca people created these patterns when they didn't have aeroplanes or even hot air balloons to be able to look down and admire them properly. Nobody really understands how or why the Nazca lines were made. It is quite a riddle!

LUNCHTIME IN ECUADOR

Ecuador is a country that sits right on the equator. The Spanish word for "equator" is *"ecuador"*. The equator is an imaginary line around the middle of the world, separating the north of the planet from the south. Tom arrived at the equator for the second time on his round-the-world adventure. He had ridden across it before in Africa.

Countries on the equator do not have different seasons, or times of the year when it gets dark very early or very late. The sun rises at about 6 o'clock in the morning and the sun sets at about 6 o'clock in the evening, every day. The weather is more or less always the same. It's usually hot.

The equator is hot because the sun shines directly overhead. (Places that are the farthest from the equator – the North Pole and the South Pole – are very cold.) When you stand on the equator you are exactly the same distance away from the North Pole as from the South Pole. You are also probably going to feel boiling hot and dream that you could be somewhere a bit colder, like the North Pole.

Have you ever noticed, when you let the water out of the bath, how the water spins down the plughole in a spiral?

If you live in the north of the world – the Northern Hemisphere, it's called – the water always spins anticlockwise. And if you live in the south of the world – the Southern Hemisphere – then the water spins clockwise as it goes down the plughole. The direction of spinning changes as you cross the equator. If only Tom ever had a bath, he would have been able to test this for himself!

Although Tom didn't miss baths, he did miss his family and always messaged them when he got the chance, sharing his stories and photos. They liked to hear from him too. But today Tom decided that he had better not send a message. His sister would not be happy with what had happened.

Because today, Tom ate a guinea pig.

And back home, Tom's sister Lucy had a pet guinea pig – Mr Squiggles. Lucy loved Mr Squiggles very much.

Tom hadn't meant to eat a guinea pig.

He felt rather guilty about eating a guinea pig. Guinea pigs are very cute.

The lady in the café had told him that lunch today was "*cuy*". Tom didn't know what *cuy* meant, but he was really hungry so he just said "yes, please – *si, por favor*".

When the *cuy* arrived at the table, Tom realised that he had just learned a new word in Spanish. An entire guinea pig, barbecued and served with chips, looked up at him unhappily from his plate. Tom tried not to think about Mr Squiggles.

But he also had to admit that the guinea pig tasted surprisingly delicious.

SPANISH WORDS

Here are some words I've learned in Spanish:

English	Spanish
Food	Comida
Water	Agua
Bread	Pan
Milk	Leche
Egg	Huevo
~~Frute~~ Fruit	Fruta
Cheese	Queso
Hello	Hola
Goodbye	Adiós
Thank you	Gracias
Please	Por favor
Guinea pig	Cuy
Gold fish	Pez dorado
Blue	Azul
Green	Verde
Yellow	Amarillo
Red	Rojo
Black	Negro
White	Blanco

Numbers 1-10

1	2	3	4	5
uno	dos	tres	cuatro	cinco
6	7	8	9	10
seis	siete	ocho	nueve	diez

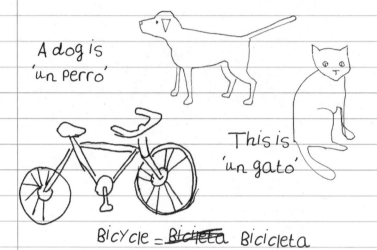

A dog is
'un perro'

This is
'un gato'

Bicycle = ~~Biciela~~ Bicicleta

Some useful phrases

MY name is ...	Me llamo ...
I am ___ years old	Tengo ___ años
I am hungry	Tengo hambre
How are you?	¿Cómo estás?
Very well, thank you	Muy bien, gracias
I like	Me gusta
I don't like	No me gusta

CYCLING
THROUGH COLOMBIA

C ycling is a popular sport in Colombia and Tom was often overtaken by speedy cyclists in proper outfits on shiny racing bikes. Usually he was faster than other people on bicycles – children on their way to school, farmers heading to market with a couple of chickens or a pig tied to the backs of their bikes – but in Colombia he felt slow and heavy as his bike was loaded down with camping gear and supplies. Riding at this snail's pace did, however, give him a chance to chat with equally slow locals. Tom always enjoyed riding side-by-side with other cyclists and finding out more about the country he was in.

One sunny morning, Pedro and Maria were cycling to the market to do some shopping for their mum when Tom caught them up.

"*¡Hola!*" called Tom.

"*¡Hola!*" replied the boy and girl. "*¿Cómo estás?* How are you?"

"*Muy bien, gracias.* Very well, thank you! *¿Cómo te llamas?* What is your name?"

"*Me llamo Pedro*. I'm called Pedro. *Maria es mi hermana* – my sister."

"*Me llamo Tom*" replied Tom. "I'm cycling round the world, *alrededor del mundo*."

The children laughed. Cycling to the shops sounded easy compared to cycling round the world.

"Isn't is dangerous? A bit crazy? *¿Un poco loco?*" asked Maria.

Now it was Tom's turn to laugh. So often when he told people about his adventures they would ask exactly the same question. Tom thought back over his journey and how often people had treated him kindly. A few people think every country in the world is scary. Most people think that a few spots are dangerous. And *everyone* always wanted to offer advice.

"Don't go to that country!" he would hear. "It is *very* dangerous."

"Watch out for the people there – they are all robbers."

When Tom first heard warnings like this he used to get very worried and think, "Oh dear! I don't think I should ride through there."

But over the thousands of miles he had ridden, Tom had learned that the best thing to do was to ask them a question: "Have you been to that country yourself?" Almost always the person had to admit that he or she had never actually been there and so really didn't know what they were talking about.

THE BOY WHO BIKED THE WORLD

Tom remembered Sergeant Sharif and Sergeant Amarri – border guards in two different African countries who had stood staring suspiciously across a border gate at each other for years. Tom had persuaded them to have a chat with each other, and they became good friends. So he was used to people thinking that the world was more dangerous than it really is. The reason that he laughed especially loudly when Maria asked if his adventure was dangerous was because they were in Colombia. Of all the countries that Tom visited in South America, nothing had got people more worried than Colombia. For many years it has had lots of problems and been known as a place to avoid.

Tom explained this to Pedro and Maria. "Everyone told me that Colombia was dangerous! They told me I should not visit."

"Colombia's not dangerous!" cried the two children together. They were pedalling up a steep hill at the time so were all a little out of breath. "This is our country and we love it. We are good people."

When you see wars and fighting on the television news it can be hard to remember that, amongst the bad things, most people in those countries are just nice, normal people like you and me, trying their best to get on with life as peacefully as they can.

The three children arrived at a junction in the road. Tom needed to turn right – *derecho*; Maria and Pedro were going left – *izquierda*. But before they said goodbye Pedro said to Tom, "I hope you enjoy the rest of our beautiful country.

You will have a good time here. Just be careful when you get to the United States. Now that is a dangerous country. I know it is – I've seen it in the movies … ¡Adios, amigo!"

Tom laughed and waved goodbye, shaking his head. The more people he met, the more he realised how similar most of us are.

Colombia's villages were small and sleepy, often set on the bank of a clear river that ran along a bed of polished stones. Children played games outside their homes and grandparents watched from gently swinging hammocks hanging in the shade beneath banana trees. The mighty mountains of South America had shrunk to steep hills by the time Tom got to Colombia. But now, even these had faded out into hot, flat, dusty plains. Tom was getting close to the end of South America. It was an exciting moment – it meant that Tom would be halfway to Alaska!

At last, he rounded a corner and there in front of him was the sea. No more mountains to climb. No more guinea pigs to eat. He had reached the end of the continent. Nine months after dipping his fingers into the cold sea down in Patagonia, the gentle Caribbean water was a gorgeously warm end to his ride through South America.

Tom sat down on the beach next to his bike. He took off his socks and shoes and wiggled his toes in the warm sand. He was happy to have reached the ocean once again. He felt proud to have ridden all the way up South America. He knew that many challenges still lay ahead, but right now it was time to celebrate. He reached into his pannier and pulled out a ready-made, double-sized banana sandwich that he had been saving especially.

Tom was a very happy boy.

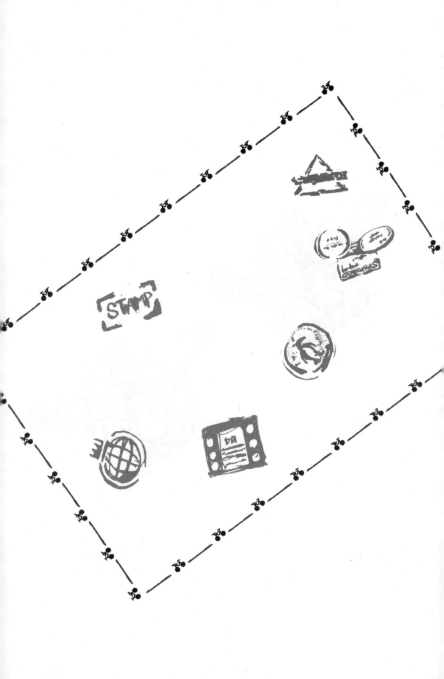

CANALS AND CROCODILES

The area where South America and North America connect is covered in dense jungle. Tall trees are packed tightly together, reaching up towards the sky. The ground is covered with undergrowth and deep swamps. Snakes curl round tangled creepers and monkeys swing high through the canopy.

Even in our modern, crowded world there are still places in the world that you can't get to by road. There are still a lot of wild places out there. The only way to move through this jungle is to hack your way through with a machete. Tom certainly could not ride through on a heavily-loaded bicycle.

Instead, he needed to sail round the jungle. Tom could then cycle from the bottom of North America up through the small Central American countries of Panama, Costa Rica, Nicaragua, Honduras, El Salvador, Guatemala and Belize. Then, after riding through Mexico, he would cross the border into the United States of America and ride north into Canada reaching – at long, long last – Alaska.

Tom set sail on a small sailing boat towards Panama.

The Panama Canal links the Atlantic Ocean and the Pacific Ocean. It is a shortcut for ships between the two oceans. Before the canal was built, ships had to sail all the way round Cape Horn at the foot of South America where Tom had ridden from: a journey of 8000 miles that took about two months in a ship. So taking a day to sail 50 miles through a canal is a much better alternative for ships! Cape Horn is also very dangerous because of the wild and stormy seas down there. Tom was looking forward to sailing through the canal – the world feels very different from a boat.

After the crossing, though, he couldn't wait to get back on his bike, his favourite place. The weather was hot and sunny. But each afternoon at about 3 o'clock, clouds began to build in the sky – big black thunderclouds. Tom knew what was about to happen. He was going to get very wet! As if on cue, the first raindrops fell. In moments the rain was harder than any Tom had ever seen. It bounced on the road and rattled on the roofs of cars. Passing traffic splashed through puddles, spraying Tom with even more water. It was good fun. And the tropical rain was nice and warm.

He was soaked to the skin in seconds. Tom's equipment was wrapped safely inside plastic bags to stay dry, but his body and clothes were as wet as if he had just stood, fully dressed, under a shower. In fact, these were Tom's showers. He didn't get the chance to wash very often, so these rainstorms were a chance to clean up a little. If you want to cycle around the world you have to get used to being a bit smelly!

THE BOY WHO BIKED THE WORLD

Under some trees, three boys sheltered from the rain. As Tom passed, they held an enormous lizard up in the air. The lizard's feet were tied together to stop it running away. The boys had caught the lizard in the jungle and now were trying to sell it to someone to keep as a pet. Dangling by its back legs, the lizard didn't look very happy at being taken out of the jungle. Tom felt sorry for the lizard. But he also knew that these boys were really poor and that in many places in the world it is hard to earn enough money to live on.

But Tom didn't think that a lizard would be the most sensible pet to take with him on his journey round the world, so he just waved at the boys and kept on riding into the rain. Just then the rain stopped, as suddenly as it had begun. The clouds disappeared and the sun came out. The road steamed as it dried in the sunshine. And Tom steamed too as *he* dried out! This mixture of sunshine and rain is why plants grow so well in tropical parts of the world.

Lots of rain also means lots of rivers. The road ran close to the sea so the rivers were wide and slow as they neared the end of their journey. On the right side of the road was jungle. The jungle was hot, green, dark and noisy with squeaking, roaring, clicking, singing creatures. On the left hand side, the roaring green waves of the Pacific Ocean smashed onto a thin sandy beach.

Tom enjoyed stopping on bridges and peering down into the water below. If he looked carefully he often spotted crocodiles! They lay half-submerged and very still.

They looked just like logs in the river. Tom did not know whether the crocodiles were sleeping or waiting to catch their lunch. Whichever one it was, he was not going to take the risk of going for a swim!

The days were hot and sweaty. Tom could not cool off by swimming in rivers like he usually did because of the crocodiles. Instead he would treat himself to a drink of refreshing sugarcane juice when he reached a village. The sugar that we use at home comes originally from a woody plant like bamboo, called sugarcane. In every village someone would be selling the juice, squeezed from the cane through a mangle and served with ice and a squeezed lemon. It was delicious!

THE PANAMA CANAL

The Panama Canal is one of the most fantastic things I've seen so far!

Here are a few facts I've learned about the canal:

- It is 48 miles long, took 10 years to dig and 25,000 people died working on it.
- The workers dug out enough earth to have built 63 massive pyramids like the ones I saw back in Egypt.
- The canal is really busy - about 40 ships pass through every day of the year.
- When a ship is crossing, a system of locks lifts the ship 26 metres above sea level.
- Ships have to pay a fee according to how big they are. The most expensive cost $375,600.
- The cheapest toll ever paid was by Richard Halliburton who swam the canal in 1928. He paid just 36¢!

PETS

After seeing the lizard in Panama today, I had a fun daydream about which pet would be the best for me ...

DOGS love running alongside bikes and would enjoy the exercise. But it might be a bit unfair to say "let's go for a bike ride" and then set off around the world!

CATS spend too much time sleeping.

Maybe a GUINEA PIG? Maybe not!! Remember what happened to the last one I met ...

A GOLDFISH? Not a good idea!

A PARROT? It could rest on my shoulder and then fly on ahead to find a good camping spot or the right turning to take. There's also loads of colourful parrots here in the jungle so my bird wouldn't get too lonely. Is a parrot the perfect solution? I think so!

VOLCANOES, JUNGLE AND DESERT MIRAGES

Costa Rica has six active volcanoes and today, Tom was going to see one in action. When he arrived, he pitched his tent on a patch of grass at the foot of the volcano. Throughout the day, smoke spewed up into the sky. Once night fell, Tom could see that glowing molten lava splashed and spurted out of the top, creating a red and orange glow above. Rumbling sounds burst from deep down inside the heart of the Earth.

Lava is liquid rock, so hot that it has melted. The centre of our planet is filled with boiling, liquid rock. (It's called magma when it's underground, lava once it's burst through the surface.) When it finds a crack in the surface of the Earth, the lava squeezes or bursts out, over time forming a volcano. Tom shuddered as he thought ahead to all the volcanoes he would cycle past in the weeks to come – an evil dictator used to get rid of his enemies by throwing them into the bubbling craters!

Fireflies flashed in the sky around the tent as he watched the volcano's display. It is incredible that a tiny insect can make its body glow. This is how fireflies send each other messages. Tom couldn't quite work out which muscles he needed to squeeze in order to make his own bum glow!

He liked to begin as early as possible because his favourite time of day to ride the dusty jungle roads was dawn. Once the sun climbed high into the sky, the temperature rose and all the sensible animals settled down to snooze through the hot part of the day. Only one stupid animal could still be seen: a sweaty young boy called Tom! He had so many miles to ride before he arrived back home that he could not afford to spend hours and hours sleeping like the local animals.

But at dawn, the jungle was still alive. Animals and birds called from the dark, humid forest that surrounded him. It was a thrilling, wild feeling to cycle through here. Tom saw brightly coloured, poisonous tree frogs, a large hairy tarantula, brilliant toucans and a lazy hanging sloth. There was the constant racket of shrieking parrots and, noisiest of all, the howler monkeys – which are the loudest animals in the world. Their call can be heard three miles away. Once, nearby in the trees, he even heard the coughing call of a jaguar.

Tom pushed down hard on his pedals with excitement. He was in Guatemala now, on his way to Tikal, the ruins of an ancient Maya city. Like Machu Picchu, Tikal has been almost completely swallowed up by jungle. But it is much older. It is almost 2000 years old. Only a few magnificent stone pyramids still stand amongst the trees. These pyramids were like the grand churches or mosques of their time, used for worship.

Tom found it amazing to stand on top of the highest pyramid, stare around, and see nothing but jungle in all directions, while funny little animals like raccoons – called *coatimundis* – snuffled around his feet looking for food. He tried to imagine a great Maya city here but the thick jungle felt as if it had been here forever. He tried to imagine standing at the top of Big Ben, the Eiffel Tower, or the Statue of Liberty and seeing nothing spreading out below but jungle for as far as his eyes could see. Tikal was once an important city to which everyone in the region flocked. But now it had faded, declined and almost totally disappeared.

As Tom pedalled north into Mexico the jungle disappeared, too, and gave way to desert. The road also improved. It was a joy to ride on smooth tarmac again; cycling feels so fast and quiet on a good road. The hot black road shimmered in the heat in the Sonora Desert, the hottest desert in North America. Roadrunner birds scampered to and fro. Snakes basked on the road, absorbing the warmth into their bodies. As he cycled past they slithered in S-shaped curves away from his wheels into the safety of the desert. Off in the distance, mirages teased young Tom. They looked like delicious lakes. He dreamed of dunking his head and drinking as much cold water as he could, as he was very hot and sweaty and thirsty.

"It's too hot!" Tom complained (forgetting his promise in Patagonia never ever to complain about the heat again!)

He pedalled on, dreaming of jumping into a lake with all his clothes on. But there was not any water out here at all, only mirages. Tom had to ration his drinking water carefully. He wished he could tip a whole bottle of water over his head, but he knew that he had to save it for drinking. He thought about how much water he wasted at home – having a shower for ages or brushing his teeth with the tap running. Out in the desert, every drop of water counts.

Whenever he came across a small village, Tom stocked up on bananas and *tortillas*. *Tortillas*, made from corn, are the Mexican version of bread, round and flat like a pancake. Wrapped around a banana they make a good Mexican-style banana sandwich! Tom toasted his *tortillas* on small campfires amongst columns of tall, spiky cacti. Shadows from the fires flickered across the dark desert floor.

As much as he loved banana *tortillas*, Tom also liked the delicious chicken *tacos* that are sold in every village in Mexico. He wanted to make them when he got back to England, so he copied down this recipe:

INGREDIENTS:
- Thin strips of chicken breast
- Thinly sliced onion, red and green peppers, tomatoes
- Garlic, red chilli, coriander and lemon juice
- *Tortillas*

Fry the chicken, onion and peppers in a hot pan with a little olive oil.

Make the *salsa* (the best bit) by chopping up, really small, red onion, green pepper, tomatoes, coriander and chilli. Mix it all up and squeeze on some lemon juice and a little olive oil.

Once the chicken is cooked, pop it all into a *tortilla*, fold it carefully in half, and eat your taco!

If you are brave, add extra slices of chilli, or a big dollop of *guacamole* (avocado mushed up with onion, chilli and oil).

Delicious! *Sabroso!*

Even though there was a proper road in Mexico, the desert was gruelling to ride through, because the days were so very long and hot. But at night it was cold, and ice formed on the outside of the tent, so the nights here were tough as well. As Tom sat huddled beside his campfire, he noticed that the moon in the sky was growing a little smaller each night. By the time the moon was new again he would be in the United States of America. This was the biggest country on his journey so far, and he was excited to go and explore it for himself.

CENTRAL AMERICA AND MEXICO

Between South America and arriving in the USA I have ridden through ⑧ countries quite quickly. Here's a few things I've learned about them:

- Panama: the Panama Canal cuts right across the whole country, connecting the Atlantic and the Pacific oceans.

- Costa Rica: You need to learn to say "pura vida" as people say it all the time for "hello" "goodbye" and "I'm OK". It means pure life or life is great! Pura vida is their way of life. Costa Rica is a happy country!

  Pura vida!

- Nicaragua: has the most active volcanoes (8) in the region.

- El Salvador: uses American dollars for its money. $ $ $

- Honduras: has one of my favourite-sounding capital cities in the world - Tegucigalpa!

● Guatemala: the money in Guatemala is named after a bird - the quetzal. In ancient times this bird's colourful feathers were used as money.

● Belize: the only country in the region where people speak English. In all the other countries, people speak Spanish. The barrier reef running down the coast of Mexico, Belize and Honduras is the second biggest coral reef in the world.

● Mexico: the world's smallest dog 'the chihuahua' originally came from Mexico. Mexico city is one of the biggest cities in the world. It's built on the site of an old dried-up lake, and the city is now sinking into it by a few centimetres every year. It introduced chocolate to the world. Mexican children don't get presents on Christmas Day. Instead they have to wait until January 6th (the day when the Three Wise Men are said to have reached Jesus).

HOLLYWOOD AND GIANT REDWOODS

Crossing from Mexico into the United States of America was a shock. Tom was used to crossing borders – showing his passport, getting it stamped, riding into the next country. But the USA felt different. People spoke English, which made life easier, even though Tom had learned quite a bit of Spanish. But the real shock was being in a rich country. America was the richest country that Tom had cycled through for a long, long time – since Europe at the beginning of his ride.

As he cycled through the USA, Tom looked around in amazement. All the roads were smooth, even the ones through small villages! There were road signs at junctions! Taps had safe drinking water! Shops had food for sale!

These things had felt normal to Tom before he began cycling round the world. But now that he had seen so many poor countries, he had learned to appreciate things that didn't used to seem important.

In most countries people looked at Tom cycling past on a bike with his panniers attached, and thought,

"Look at that boy! He has a bike and all those bags. He must be really rich!"

Now, in the USA, people looked at Tom and thought,

"Look at that boy! All he has is a bike and those few bags. He must be really poor."

Tom didn't care if he was rich or poor. He felt like the richest person in the world because he was out having a brilliant adventure and spending his days doing something that he loved.

Quite a lot of the USA looked familiar, even though Tom had never been here before. This is because American films, television, cartoons, comics and music are so common around the world. As he cycled along, he kept spotting tiny details of American life that made him feel as though he was cycling through a film set rather than it being real life. He saw yellow school buses like on TV, post boxes on stands at the bottom of people's gardens, doughnut shops and the police cars he was used to seeing chasing bad guys across town!

In shops Tom would spot items of food and think excitedly to himself, "They have English food here!" But, in fact, many of the things Tom enjoyed eating at home – breakfast cereals, fizzy drinks, ketchup, hot dogs, burgers – all came to England from the USA.

As Tom cycled through Arizona, he was looking forward to reaching the Grand Canyon, one of the most famous sights in the world. The Grand Canyon was formed over millions of years by the waters of the Colorado River. Slowly, slowly the river wore down the rock, carving out an enormous canyon. The canyon is 200 miles long and over a mile deep. The rock at the bottom of the canyon is much older than the rock at the surface. At the bottom, the rock is almost 2 billion years old (2,000,000,000 years)!

It is no surprise that the Grand Canyon is the most popular tourist destination in the state of Arizona. What is more surprising is the *second* most popular tourist destination in Arizona: London Bridge! About 50 years ago this famous old bridge from the River Thames in England was bought by an American and shipped, brick by brick, across the ocean to the USA. Instead of battling a cold and rainy climate, it now stands across the Colorado River in hot and dusty Arizona. The bridge looked a bit odd so far away from home out under the blue desert skies.

In California, the desert gradually gave way to green fields and palm trees. Snow-covered mountains shone in the distance as Tom rode towards the ocean and Los Angeles. He huffed and puffed his way up the hills above the city to take a photo of himself in front of the famous HOLLYWOOD sign. Tom smiled as he sent the picture to his little sister back home. She dreamed of being an actress and starring in one of the famous films they make in Hollywood.

But Tom wasn't crazy about all the traffic in Los Angeles and the fumes coming out of the fancy cars so he rode on up the coast, heading for San Francisco. The hills in that city are not very long – nothing at all compared to the Andes. But they *were* the steepest roads Tom had ever ridden. (This is because mountain roads zig-zag, but city streets go straight up into the air without curving. Steep city streets can be very hard work!)

Tom had to share the roads in San Francisco with trams. These run on rails, like a train, in amongst all the normal cars and buses. There are poles on the trams so that standing passengers can hold on to the outside of the tram during busy periods when there is no space left inside. The people travelling on the outside of the trams would cheer at Tom as they overtook him up a ridiculously steep street. They cheered but they could not clap as they would have fallen off!

Tom wanted to visit Alcatraz, the famous high-security prison on an island in the bay off San Francisco. Alcatraz is where the toughest and most dangerous criminals used to be kept, including the famous gangster Al Capone. The prison cells were tiny: a prisoner could stretch his arms out and touch both walls at once. It was almost impossible for a prisoner to escape from Alcatraz. Today, though, the prison has closed down and it's just a tourist attraction.

As Tom cycled over the Golden Gate Bridge, he looked down at the tiny prison island. From up high on the bridge, about 75 metres above the water, Tom could understand why Alcatraz used to be so feared by criminals. Alcatraz was more than a mile out to sea and surrounded by cold and dangerous water.

The Golden Gate Bridge is one of the most famous landmarks in the world. Tom had already seen its famous curves and distinctive orange colour in countless photographs. But it's always better to see things for yourself. When it was built, this was the longest suspension bridge in the world. The whole weight of the road is suspended from two enormous cables. The cables are over 2000 metres long and almost a metre thick!

After crossing the Golden Gate, Tom followed Highway 1, which hugs the Pacific Ocean on a winding, cliff-edge road. On his right hand side were vineyards and fields of flowers. On his left was the shining ocean. Each night Tom climbed down to the beach to camp. He watched the sun setting over the ocean from the open door of his tent and listened to elephant seals grunting noisily beside the water. This was one of Tom's favourite ever roads.

One of the highlights were the forests of giant redwood trees. Giant redwoods are really beautiful trees. They usually grow about 80 metres tall, though the tallest of all is 115 metres. They live for 2000 years, and weigh as much as 2000 tonnes! Giant redwoods are the tallest trees in the world.

One of the redwoods in northern California is so large that a hole has been cut through the middle of it so that people can drive through it, just for fun. Can you imagine how big a tree needs to be in order to drive a car through it?! Tom grinned as he cycled through the tree. This adventure was so full of surprises.

Cycling through the USA felt a bit like a holiday to Tom. It was beautiful, it was fun, it was easy. He enjoyed it very much. But he wasn't trying to cycle round the world because he wanted to take it easy. He was trying to cycle round the world because he wanted strange and surprising cultures, and because he wanted huge, empty, adventurous wilderness and big, difficult challenges. So he rode on quickly towards Canada and Alaska. Tom was about to really head into the wild!

USA FACTS

The USA is one of the biggest and most important countries I've cycled through. Here are a few things I've learned about it:

- The USA is quite a young country. It only became independent on July 4th 1776 when it split away from Great Britain.

- The USA (or United States of America) is made up of 50 states. This is why there are 50 stars on the American flag.

- Alaska is the biggest state and Rhode Island is the smallest state. The state of California is bigger by itself than 85 of the world's countries.

- Two of the states - Hawaii and Alaska - are separated by land or by sea from all of the other states.

- Alaska was bought from Russia in 1867. Hawaii joined the union of other states in 1959.

- Only American people have ever walked on the moon.

- Death Valley, in the Mojave desert in eastern California, is the hottest place in the world. Its record highest temperature was 57°c. It is so hot that you can fry an egg without a cooker!

- The national bird of the USA is the bald eagle. A bald eagle has a beautiful white head and a hooked yellow beak. It can see a fish for a mile away and dive at 100mph when hunting!

(Good picture, hey? Drawn by someone I met in the USA!)

THE SEA-TO-SKY
HIGHWAY

Tom couldn't believe the size of Canada. It is the second biggest country in the world. Towns might be hundreds of miles apart, roads run on and on and on for week after week without any change of scenery. Wherever Tom looked, trees stretched off forever into the distance. He wondered how many trees there were in Canada. Sometimes he would cycle, counting as he went along: one, two, tree …

To Tom, who had grown up in the small and crowded landscape of England, the vast emptiness was unbelievably exciting. The world felt enormous and wild and undisturbed. He was on a road called the Sea-to-Sky Highway. Cycling from sea to sky sounded as though it was going to be a lot of hard work! He rode through forests, past lakes and waterfalls and across cold rivers. Tom saw moose, deer, beavers, bald eagles, foxes and coyotes. Then, one evening, he saw his first black bear. A mother bear and two cubs grazed in a field of long grass. Tom stood still and watched, nervous and fascinated. These were the biggest, wildest animals he had seen since Africa. He was careful not to get too close or to make any sudden movements that might scare the bears.

One night Tom heard rustling sounds right outside his tent. He sat straight up, eyes wide with fright. He was sure a bear was snuffling round right outside; it was probably sniffing him. He thought he was going to be eaten at any moment. Tom didn't think he'd taste very delicious, but maybe bears think differently. There was nothing that he could do, he was stuck inside the tent. His heart beat faster.

Tom was very scared. Bears are much bigger than humans. They'll only attack humans if they are threatened or very hungry. If this bear was hungry, then Tom was in big trouble. He could not see the snarling head and the giant teeth and drooling mouth, but he could imagine them. And imagining is almost worse! Eventually he could not stand the uncertainty any longer. Time to come face to face with his fate. Tom carefully eased the zip on the tent door. The beast was just outside, only inches away from his face. The animal that had turned Tom into a wobbling jelly of terror. Right there, in front of Tom's face was … a tiny little bird, hopping around in the leaves! He laughed, feeling very silly indeed. The bird flew away in fright as soon as it saw the giant human boy!

Although Tom loved Canada, he hated the mornings in Canada. The mosquitoes in summertime are perhaps the worst in the world. Whenever Tom stopped cycling he was mobbed by clouds of them. They whined and whirred around his face, covering every patch of bare skin and sucking his blood. Tom swatted them and whirled his arms around his head, but it was no good. There were too many. The only ways to escape from the itchy torture were either to cycle so fast that the horrid little monsters could not keep up, or to fling up his tent as fast as possible and dive inside, zipping the door behind him. The first sight each morning was horrible. Through the thin fabric of the tent, Tom could see the outline of hundreds of mosquitoes. They could smell the juicy, tasty boy inside but they could not get close enough to suck his blood. So they sat patiently on the outside of his tent, waiting for him to come out and serve them breakfast.

This was a terrible way for a day to begin. Tom hated mosquitoes. The red itchy bites. The insect clouds in his eyes and nose and mouth. The high-pitched screaming sound in his ears. Before he could jump on his bike and escape, he knew that he had to climb out and face the evil little army.

He got dressed, ate breakfast and brushed his teeth inside the tent. Then he had to jump out, waving his arms wildly, flapping and slapping his body as the insects swooped. Like a mad man, Tom pulled down the tent as fast as he could. He shoved it into a pannier, jumped on his bike, and rode as fast as his legs could carry him. The cloud of chasing mosquitoes could not keep up, and at last Tom would escape them and be able to relax a bit. It was an annoying, itchy beginning to each day. But at least it helped him get ready really quickly!

At home, Tom's Dad was always nagging at him to hurry up and get ready for school. Now, without his Dad to nag him, Tom was actually ready faster than ever before.

The Yukon is one of the emptiest regions in Canada. It is twice as big as Great Britain, but there are 2000 times as many people living in Britain! Up until 120 years ago, there were no towns in the Yukon at all. People have been here for thousands of years, but they always lived in small groups, moving around in search of better hunting and fishing. They were nomads. Life was tough, but simple.

The native people were very good hunters and clever at building different kinds of shelters, such as wigwams, teepees and igloos. They made clothes from animal hides and fur. They hunted animals and gathered and grew plants. They built canoes out of birch bark and caught fish using spears, nets and traps. But in 1896, everything changed. And it changed fast. One word transformed a way of life that had existed for hundreds of years.

That word was GOLD!

In 1896, Skookum Jim Mason, Kate Carmack and her husband George discovered enormous gold deposits in Bonanza Creek in the Yukon. Searching for gold is a hard life most of the time. Can you imagine searching for gold and day after day finding nothing but stones? You're poor and bored and hungry. The mosquitoes are driving you crazy. Every day you think about giving up. Every evening you persuade yourself to try again, just one more time.

And then, one ordinary day, you spot something shiny, glinting in the sun. At first you don't believe what you are seeing. Gold! A pebble-sized chunk of solid gold! It really is gold! And then you spot another. And then another! Their luck had changed. Jim, Kate and George were suddenly rich beyond their wildest imaginations!

It doesn't take long for news like this to spread. The lucky three tried to keep it a secret, but word of their discovery soon reached the cities further south, and the stampede began. Tens of thousands of people rushed north to the Yukon, desperate for gold, greedy to be rich. The Gold Rush had begun!

The crowds travelled by ship from the cities of the west coast of the USA. Then their struggles really began. The early prospectors had to be extremely determined even to make it as far as the Yukon. There were no roads or maps or shops. You had to make your own way cross-country, carrying everything, and you had to be able to survive once you arrived. They had to battle up and over a snowy mountain pass and down to the Yukon River. Every person needed to bring with them a year's supply of food. Think about how much food you'd need for a whole year ...

Once they reached the broad river, the excited gold hunters then had to build a raft and paddle downstream for 500 miles. To build their rafts, the gold hunters chopped down trees and lashed the trunks together. The rafts were huge, in order to carry all the food and equipment, and all the trees were stripped from the land. Everybody was in a rush to race down the river, and competition was fierce to be one of the first to arrive at the places where gold had been found. In winter the river was frozen solid, so travel was impossible. As soon as the ice thawed in the springtime, hundreds of rafts launched down the wild, cold river. Many people drowned or sank or capsized on the dangerous journey.

So many people raced to the Gold Rush area that a new town sprang up, Dawson City. Many people arrived to discover that the best gold areas had already been taken. They returned home, sad and disappointed, having spent all their money on the gamble for gold. A few people *did* return clutching heavy bags of shining gold, but many did not.

Tom was thrilled by these tales of the Gold Rush. And since he was there, he decided to give it a go himself. The simplest way to search for gold is called "panning". So one evening after washing up his cooking pan, he scooped gravel and water from the river into his pan. Then he shook it from side to side, keeping a steady rhythm. Because gold is heavier than gravel, it sinks to the bottom of a pan, separating the shiny, valuable gold from the worthless stones. Sadly, Tom didn't find any gold. But as he tucked his pan away, he realised he didn't care. He didn't need to become a millionaire. A life filled with adventure, nature, wilderness and challenges felt like a life rich enough for him.

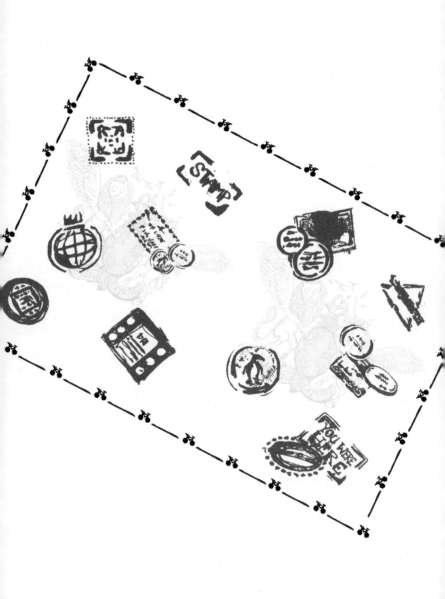

THE TOM-TIKI

Smoke! Tom smelled smoke. Then he saw it – flakes of ash falling from the sky, like black snow. It tickled his nostrils. It made him cough. Summer in the Yukon is fire season. The forests dry out over the warm summer months, and when there is a thunderstorm, lightning bolts can start a fire. Because the wood is dry, these forest fires grow and spread quickly. They become so large that it's impossible for the fire brigade to put them out.

The only thing to do is to wait for the fires to go out by themselves, either because they run out of wood to burn through or because the wind changes direction and stops blowing the fire towards new areas of forest. Tom arrived in a small town, wanting to find out more about the fire. The fire was north of him – the direction he needed in order to cycle to Alaska. He asked a policeman what was happening.

"This fire is one of the worst we've had in the Yukon," the policeman said. "At the moment it covers an area bigger than 2 million football pitches."

"Wow!" Tom gasped. He thought about how big a fire that covered even one football pitch would look. It was hard to imagine a fire covering *2 million* pitches … Another way to imagine the size of this fire is that it was as big as Wales! He was really worried about his journey now. He asked the policeman for advice.

"I'm afraid it doesn't look good," he said. "This fire will be burning for a long time, and the only road to Alaska goes straight through the middle of it. It's not going to be possible to continue your ride. I'm sorry. You'll have to give up and go home."

Tom's heart sank. He had cycled so far. Surely his quest to become the boy who biked the world wasn't going to fail now? But if he could not continue down the road then his adventure could not continue. His plans had fallen apart. He had failed. Tom was so disappointed he almost started to cry.

"Cheer up!" said the policeman, when he saw that Tom was upset. "You'll find a way. Roads are new things up here in the Yukon. It's not so long ago that there weren't any roads at all. And people travelled around just fine. Do you know how they did it back then?"

"By river?" guessed the boy. Apart from the roads and rivers, everywhere else up here was totally covered in thick forest.

"Exactly! In the winter the rivers freeze as solid as concrete. Folk used the frozen rivers to travel along just like a road …"

" … but it's the middle of summer! I can't cycle down a river!" interrupted Tom, who was really annoyed at the thought of his expedition grinding to a halt.

"No, you can't pedal down a river," agreed the policeman, patiently. "But you can *paddle* …"

At just the same moment, Tom and the policeman smiled and nodded their heads. The best adventures are the ones that sneak up on you without warning, the mad and exciting ideas that spring into your mind from nowhere. If you are brave enough to try new things and go to new places, then these are the best experiences to have.

"I can paddle downstream until I get past the fires! I'll travel by raft!" Tom exclaimed, excitement in his voice and with eyes sparkling. "That's a brilliant idea!"

Now that *did* sound like an adventure!

The Yukon River is the largest river in the Yukon and Alaska. It's almost 2000 miles long. Tom worked out that he would have to paddle for 500 miles before he was safely past the fires and could get back on his bike again.

The River Yukon flows through the town of Whitehorse. Tom began to build his raft here. He bought a saw then headed into the nearby forest to cut long, straight logs. It was hard work, sawing away, then hauling the wood back to the riverbank. But it was thrilling, too. Starting a new project is always exciting, doing something new, something difficult, something with lots to learn from. Tom whistled as he worked. Local people in Whitehorse heard about the boy who was trying to travel the whole way round the world. They came down to the riverbank to watch him build his raft.

Some thought he was brave. Many thought he was crazy. Most had words of warning and tried to put him off the idea.

"The river's too high …"

"The river's too cold …"

"The bears will get you …"

"The fires will get you …"

"You'll sink if you load your bike onto that raft …"

But Tom was used to people trying to put him off hatching adventurous plans. He remembered being surrounded by children in the school playground, laughing when he told them that he was going to bike around the world. They called him a silly daydreamer. Tom *was* a daydreamer, that much was true. Everyone daydreams. But not equally. Those daydreamers who actually get out the door and make their dreams real are the ones who become adventurers.

He knew there were risks in adventure. He thought about them before he began and he took care. But if you want to do difficult, exciting things in life then you have to carefully but regularly test what you are really able to do. You have to learn to think whether a risk is worth taking, or if it is just silly. You need to figure out *how* to take a risk, so that it doesn't hurt you. And you need to be brave, trying out things that you previously felt might be too hard. If you do these things often, you'll start to understand that you are capable of more that you ever imagined. You really are. We all are.

After days of hard work Tom was tired, but the raft was almost finished. He had tied several logs together, making a raft big enough for both himself and his bike. He could sleep on it, too. Tom made oars from wood, and stocked up with food (lots of bananas) and drinking water. A crowd of people helped him launch the heavy raft into the water and tie down the bike and equipment. Then they gave the raft a big push out into the river. He was off!

"Three cheers!" they shouted, smiling and waving. "Good luck!"

Although the crowd had been warning Tom about all the things that might go wrong, they knew that mostly they had just been giving themselves excuses as to why they were not going on exciting trips like Tom. They were all actually a bit jealous as the raft drifted out into the current and began floating merrily down the stream.

"Hip, hip hooray!"

Tom was very proud of his raft. He thought that it deserved a name. He decided to call his raft the *Tom-Tiki*. He had no map of the river, but then neither did any of the brave early explorers who rushed here seeking gold. At least he knew that somewhere down the river there would eventually be a town. And he was on his way!

Tom pulled hard on the oars. The *Tom-Tiki* was enormous, and working the oars was difficult. It didn't take long to become red and sweaty and for his arms to ache. When he got tired on his bike he would just stop riding and sit down for a rest. So he decided to try the same thing on the river.

He put down the oars. And that was the moment that Tom really, really began to enjoy his rafting adventure. Because even when he was not rowing, the raft kept moving, pushed downstream by the river current. He realised that, unlike cycling, on a raft you can just relax and you will still keep moving. It was a very easy way to have an adventure. He settled into some serious lying down and relaxing. This was the life! Yukon Ho!

For 10 days Tom travelled down the river aboard the *Tom-Tiki*, drifting around the edges of the forest fire. Sometimes there were islands. He either steered around them or, if it was late in the afternoon, tied the raft to a tree and stepped onto the island to camp. Camping on an island is really fun, something Tom could never do when he was on his bike. He also liked the islands because being on an island felt a little bit safer than the riverbank from the bears he saw daily.

Moose sometimes swam across the water with only their heads showing. Their huge ears were pinned back as they strained against the current. A beaver swam towards its jumbled lodge of branches and mud. Scared by Tom's approach, the beaver slapped the water with his tail and disappeared in a dive down into his underwater home. Bald eagles sat in treetops watching the world and looking for fish. Above the water, colourful dragonflies hovered and whirred. And under the water were racing, muscular salmon, but Tom never managed to catch one for his tea.

He did not see another person, road or town while drifting along the river. He was alone in the wild, seeing exactly the same sights as the Gold Rush adventurers a century ago. Because Tom didn't have a map, he had no idea when he would arrive at Dawson City. He hoped that he would not miss it whilst having a little nap and end up drifting all the way to the sea!

It was a happy moment when the *Tom-Tiki* rounded a bend and there was Dawson City, hugging the right bank of the river. Tom paddled across and clambered ashore. He was excited to see people again, to sleep without being nervous about bears, and to stock up on fresh food. Once he had unloaded his gear, Tom gave the raft a push back out into the river, where it caught the current and headed downstream. The *Tom-Tiki* had a long journey ahead, drifting gently and quietly on its own, all the way to the Bering Sea. Tom was sad to see it go.

HOW TO MAKE A RAFT

It was lots of hard work and also lots of fun making a raft to paddle down the Yukon River. Here are some drawings of how to do it:

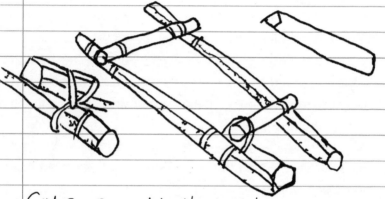

Cut some wood to the lengths you need them and tie them together.

Here's how to tie them together.

Et Voila! (I remember some of the French I learned in France, too!).

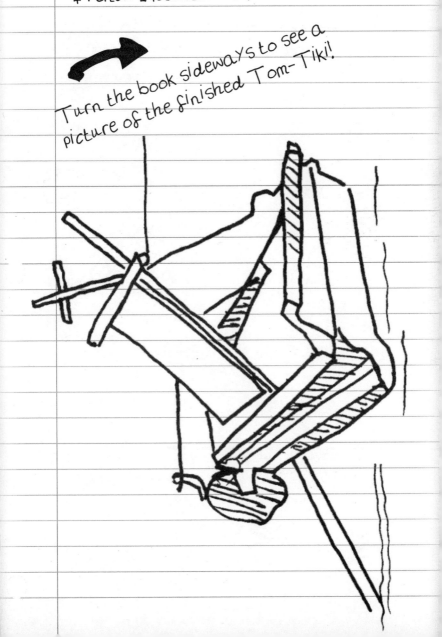

Turn the book sideways to see a picture of the finished Tom-Tiki!

ALASKA: THE FINAL ROAD TO THE MIDNIGHT SUN

It felt good to be back on the bike after the lazy days of raft-sitting and watching the world slide by. Ahead lay yet another road. But it wasn't far now. This was the final road to Alaska. The end of the Americas at last! At the thought, Tom pedalled very fast, revving up speed and singing loudly to himself. Singing loudly was not just fun, it also meant that bears would not be surprised by his sudden approach, so it helped keep him safe too.

Alaska is part of the USA even though it is separated from the rest of the country by Canada. He dug his passport from the bottom of the pannier, where he kept it safely stored. The guard looked silently through the pages of Tom's passport. There were so many different stamps in there from all the countries Tom had cycled through. When the border guard reached the last page of the passport, he flipped back to the beginning and studied the whole thing again. He had a strange look on his face.

Tom watched him, quietly. Was there a problem with his passport? Was the guard about to tell Tom that he could not enter Alaska? He had only just battled round the forest fire. He began to feel nervous.

The guard looked up at Tom.

"Young man," he spoke seriously. "Have you travelled all the way from Patagonia to Alaska? Have you really?"

"Yes sir," answered Tom.

"And have you come all that way on your bicycle?"

"Yes sir. And on a sailing boat and a raft."

"Well, in that case, I think you had better come inside and have a great big piece of cake. Congratulations! Welcome to Alaska!"

Tom was a very happy boy. His journey through the Americas was almost complete. And he loved cake. This was a good day!

Alaska is absolutely huge. You can fit the whole of Great Britain easily into Alaska, yet there are only about as many people living in Alaska as in the town of Leeds in England. So Tom still had a long way to ride. He was going to ride to the far north, all the way to where the road ran into the Arctic Ocean. He wanted to cycle until there was no more road to ride.

Tom loved the ride along that long empty road, remembering how many months it had taken to get here from Patagonia. He thought about all the people who had helped him get this far. He remembered the times when it had seemed too hard or too far or too hot or too cold, and how close he had come to quitting. He felt proud to have kept going.

Everywhere in the world (except on the equator), the sun sets later in summer than in winter. The further away from the equator, the lighter the summer evenings become. The sun sets later each evening and rises earlier each morning. As Tom headed further and further north, the sun was setting so late that he usually went to sleep before it even set. And dawn came so early that he would wake up to bright sunshine streaming into his tent.

Eventually, heading north, you cross a line where on the longest day of the year, the sun never sets. This line is called the Arctic Circle. On June 21st, the summer solstice, the sun doesn't drop below the horizon at all. It just goes round and round the sky. It never gets dark. The night that Tom crossed the Arctic Circle he sat outside his tent writing in his diary and reading his book until very late. He wanted to enjoy the midnight sun and watch the sun sliding low across the sky but not actually sinking out of sight. When you cycle round the world you can stay up until midnight anytime you want: you don't have your Mum or Dad to make you go to bed!

The boy loaded his bags with enough food to last for 10 days. Ten days was how long it would take to reach the Arctic Ocean and there would not be anywhere on the way to buy supplies. But the end of the Americas was almost in sight! The hills were steep and he had to push as hard as he could on the pedals to keep moving up the track. Sweat poured down his face, mixing with dust until he was absolutely filthy. It was tough work, but Tom enjoyed the way Alaska was throwing up a final challenge. He didn't want the end to be easy. He wanted to earn his reward. Even the downhills were tricky. He couldn't zoom down them like he usually did because there was a big risk of skidding and crashing on the loose gravel.

Tom cycled past Mount McKinley (also called Mount Denali), at 6194 metres the highest mountain in North America. He was boiling hot, but the mountain itself was covered in snow. It was an impressive sight. Maybe one day he'd come back and climb that mountain, he thought. He had now cycled alongside the highest mountains in Africa (Kilimanjaro – 5895m), South America (Aconcagua – 6960m) and North America.

Sheep scrambled high above on the scree slopes; caribou and muskox grazed on the valley's grass; and yet another grizzly bear trotted across the road. Approaching the last big climb over the Brooks mountain range – called the Atigun Pass – Tom passed the final tree. From here all the way to the North Pole there were no more trees: the weather was too harsh for them to grow this far north. After this mountain pass, for thousands of miles in every direction, was nothing but flat, boggy grassland, called tundra. The small, deserted road would lead Tom towards the ocean and the end of North America. He rode for days, thinking back over all the adventures he had had, until one exciting day, ahead of him, he spied the grey waters of Prudhoe Bay.

He had done it! He was there! Tom pushed his bike down to the water's edge, ready to celebrate in his favourite way: a double-sized banana sandwich. This was followed by a quick swim in the Arctic Ocean. It was a very quick swim because it was freezing cold and because polar bears are often seen around here. He didn't want his celebration to end by becoming lunch for a polar bear!

Tom was amazed that he had just ridden 17,848 kilometres – all the way from that signpost at the bottom of Patagonia to the very top of Alaska. It was so far for one boy to have ridden! And he had been so worried.

Here, though, is Tom's secret, the secret that can make any normal boy or girl do something really amazing. Tom had a big dream – to cycle all the way up the Americas as part of his adventure round the world. Having a big dream is important.

But just having a dream is not enough. Tom also did the most important thing of all – he began. He started small: just climbing onto his bike and starting to pedal north. That's easy, it's tiny, anyone can do it. But it's also the hardest thing of all: thinking small so as not to put yourself off, starting small, but making sure you actually begin. The rest will follow little by little.

Think big. But start small.

And, with that, Tom settled down on the pebble beach beside the Arctic Ocean to treat himself to one more banana sandwich. He had ridden a long way now – from his home all the way through Africa and now up the Americas. But he knew that there was a long way to go before he arrived back home again. He still had to cycle all the way across Asia before he became the boy who biked the world …

The Boy Who Biked The World: Riding Home

Keep up with Tom as he cycles across Asia on the final leg of his adventure round the world. Skid along as he cycles through the snows of Siberia. With temperatures dropping as low as -40 degrees (much colder than a freezer), you'll be shivering as you read.

Smile as Tom relaxes in a steaming hot pool in Japan, sharing his bath with some surprised monkeys! Discover the weird and wonderful foods of China - foods that you definitely won't find in your local Chinese Takeaway!

Join Tom as he follows the Great Wall of China towards the mysterious lands of Central Asia where he will encounter the Gates of Hell, craters in the desert that blaze with fire day and night. He'll have to find a way across the world's largest inland sea before he can get back to Europe. And, of course, he'll be eating his favourite banana sandwiches wherever he goes!

As always, Tom will discover strange and amazing sights. He'll meet a host of fun characters, and learn lots about the cultures and countries of the world along the way.

Share Tom's excitement as the end of his adventure draws closer as he arrives back in England and pedals back towards his friends, his family, and all the people in his school who never believed that Tom could ever cycle round the world.

YOUR JOURNAL

Plan your own adventure here!

What's your dream adventure? Where
in the world would you like to go and
why?

Think about how you would like to
travel there. And don't forget to write
your kit list.

YOUR JOURNAL

What would you like to see and experience?
Perhaps you'd like to see pandas or
experience the heat of a desert.

What would You need to be mindful
of while You're there? Think about
the physical environment as well as the
culture.

About Eye Books

Eye Books is a small independent publisher that passionately believes the more you put into life the more you get out of it.

It publishes stories that show ordinary people can and do achieve extraordinary things.

Its books celebrate 'living' rather than existing.

We are committed to ethical publishing and try to minimise our carbon footprint in the manufacturing and distribution of our books.

www.eye-books.com

eye books

About Extraordinary Things Done by Ordinary People

About the Author

Alastair Humphreys is an adventurer, blogger, author, motivational speaker.

Alastair's quest for adventure began young. Aged eight, he completed the Yorkshire Three Peaks challenge and at 13 he did the National Three Peaks in 24 hours! At 14 he cycled off-road across England.

At university, Alastair trained to become a teacher. But adventure took over! Alastair has now cycled round the world, raced a yacht across the Atlantic Ocean, canoed 500 miles down the Yukon River and walked the length of the holy Kaveri river in India. He has run the Marathon des Sables, crossed Iceland by foot and packraft, rowed across the Atlantic Ocean, and walked across the Empty Quarter desert.

More recently Alastair has been encouraging people to seek out adventure close to home. The 'microadventures' idea saw Alastair named as one of National Geographic's Adventurers of the Year.

Alastair is always blogging and tweeting about his adventures, big and small. Visit his website www.alastairhumphreys.com to see what he is up to and follow him on social media.